KNOW ABOUT
INDIA

MAPLE KIDS

Contents

Preface

India is a vast South Asian country with diverse terrain – from Himalayan peaks to Indian Ocean coastline. It is impossible not to be astonished by India. India's rich and multi-layered cultures are dominated by religious and spiritual themes. Nowhere on Earth does humanity present itself in such an amazing heritage of cultures, religions and distinct languages. Every aspect of the country presents itself on a massive, exaggerated scale, worthy in comparison only to the superlative mountains that overshadow it. The large number of different cultures, knitted together in such a close and perfect manner, make India's diversity one of the wonders of the world.

With nearly 1.3 billion citizens, India is the second most populous nation in the world. It is impossible to speak of any one Indian culture, although there are deep cultural continuities that tie its people together. English is the major language of trade and politics, but there are twenty two official languages in all. There are twenty-four languages that are spoken by a million people or more and countless other dialects. India has seven major religions and many minor ones, six main ethnic groups and countless holidays.

This book gives a brief overview on India.

CHAPTER 1
India - Fact File

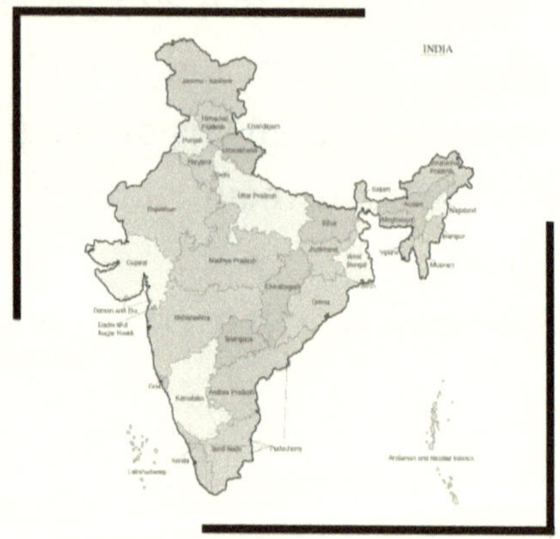

India will sideswipe you with its size, clamour and diversity. Nothing in the country is ever quite what you expect and the only thing to expect is the unexpected which comes in many forms and will always want to sit next to you. India is a litmus test for many travellers and some visitors are only too happy to get on an aircraft and fly away, but if you enjoy delving into convoluted cosmologies and thrive on sensual overload, then India is one of the most intricate and rewarding dramas unfolding on earth.

Full Country Name: Republic of India

Area: 3,287,263 km2(1,269,219 sq mi)

Population: 1.339 Billion

Capital City: New Delhi

People: 72% Indo-Aryan, 25% Dravidian, 3% other

Language: Hindi

Religion: 74.33% Hindu, 14.20% Muslim, 5.84% Christian, 1.86% Sikh, 0.82% Buddhist, 1.1% Jain, 0.47% other, 1.42 % Ethno religionist.

Government: Federal Republic

President: Ram Nath Kovind

GDP: US$ 2.454 trillion

GDP per capita: US$ 1850

Annual growth: 5.7%

Inflation: 3.36%

Major industries: Textiles, Chemicals, Food Processing, Steel, Transportation Equipment, Cement, Mining, Petroleum, Machinery, Rice, Wheat, Oilseed, Cotton, Jute, Tea, Sugarcane,

Potatoes; Cattle, Water Buffalo, Sheep, Goats, Poultry, Fish

Major trading partners: US, Hong Kong, UK, Japan. Germany, Belgium, Saudi Arabia

Facts for the traveller

Visas: Six month multiple-entry visas are now issued to most nationals regardless of whether you intend staying that long or re-entering the country.

Health risks: Cholera, dengue fever, dysentery, hepatitis, malaria, meningitis (trekking areas only) and typhoid. Many of India's larger cities are highly polluted and travellers with respiratory ailments may wish to take precautionary measures.

Time: GMT/UTC plus 5 hours 30 minutes

Electricity: 230-240V, 50 HZ

Weights & measures: Metric

When to go

India has such a wide range of climatic factors that it's impossible to pin down the best time to visit weather-wise with any certainty. Broadly speaking October to March tends to be the most pleasant months over much of the country. In the far south, the monsoonal weather pattern tends to make January to September more pleasant, while Sikkim and the areas of north-eastern India tend to be much enjoyable during March to August and Kashmir and the mountainous regions of Himachal Pradesh are at their most accessible between May and September. The deserts of Rajasthan and the north-western Indian Himalayan region are at their best during the monsoon.

The trekking season in the Indian Himalayas run roughly from April to November, though this varies widely depending on the trek, altitude and region. The ski season is between January and March, The dates of particular festivals which may determine the timing of your visit are listed in the events section.

CHAPTER 2
Festivals of India

India is blessed with a huge number of festivals and several are so spectacular that you would be an unfortunate to miss them, especially if you were remotely within the proximity. They start with the secular ***Republic Day Festival*** in Delhi each January, which includes procession of elephants, camels, horses and tableaux, spectacular display of military might and Indian princely splendour. In March arrives festival of colours –***Holi***, which is one of the most exuberant Hindu festivals in the north of India. It marks the arrival of spring and is a celebration of fertility, colour, and love, as well as the triumph of good versus evil. This festival involves throwing of coloured powders (known as gulal) on one another and getting drenched in water.

The 10-day ***Shi'ite Muharram Festival*** commemorates the martyrdom of Hussein ibn Ali, the grandson of Muhammad and son of Ali, in the Battle of Karbala. It's marked by a grand parade and dedicated penitents scourge themselves with whips in religious fervour. It is best seen in Lucknow, the principal Indian Shi'ite city and takes place in April/May for the next couple of years. The massive ***Kumbh Mela Festival*** commemorates an ancient battle between Gods and Demons for possession of a pitcher (Kumbh) filled with nectar. During this fight, four drops of nectar fell from the pitcher and landed in Allahabad, Haridwar, Nasik and Ujjain. The mela is held every three years rotating through these four cities. Kumbh Mela is a mass Hindu pilgrimage of faith in which

Hindus gather in these cities to bathe in a sacred river. The next festival will take place at Prayag (Allahabad) in 2019.

Don't mistake the great chariot festival, **Jagannath Rath Yatra** for a rally race. This spectacle in Puri (state of Odisha) in June/July involves the gigantic temple chariot of Lord Jagannath making its annual journey, pulled by thousands of eager devotees.

Every year the chariots of Lord Jagannath accompanied by his elder brother Balabhadra and sister Devi Subhadra are brought out on to the Main Street of Puri and then taken to the Shri Gundicha Temple to their aunt's house where the deities enjoy a nine days stay and return to their temple.

One of the big events of the year in Kerala is the Nehru Cup **Snake Boat Races** on the backwaters at Alappuzha (Alleppey), which takes place on the second Saturday of August every year.

The festival of **Ganesh Chaturthi** in August/ September is dedicated to the popular elephant-headed god, Lord Ganesh. The festival celebrates Lord Ganesha as the God of New Beginnings and the Remover of Obstacles and is observed throughout India but with particular enthusiasm in Maharashtra. Shrines are erected, firecrackers let off, clay idols are immersed in rivers or the sea. During Ganesh Chaturthi everyone tries to avoid looking at the moon as it is believed that the person who looks at the moon on this day will fall victim to Mithya Kalank ie., the person will be falsely accused of stealing something.

September/October is the time to head for the hills to see the delightful Festival of the Gods in Kullu, this is the part of **Dussehra Festival**. Dussehra is one of the significant Hindu festivals, celebrated over 10 days with much joy and happiness in the entire country. The occasion marks the triumph of Lord Ram over Ravana, the victory of good over evil. The nine days of Dussehra is also celebrated as Navratri wherein the three divine mothers - Goddesses Durga, Lakshmi & Saraswati are worshiped so as to attain health, wealth, prosperity and knowledge.

November is the time for the huge and colourful **Camel Festival** at Pushkar in Rajasthan. Deepawali, festival of lights is one of the most popular festivals of the Hindu calendar, it spiritually signifies the victory of light over darkness, good over evil, knowledge over ignorance, and hope over despair. This festival falls in October/November. Deepawali is celebrated by lighting large number of candles and oil lamps in housetops and other premises, followed by firecrackers & sweet distribution among families.

Now comes December, the month of Christmas celebrations. Goa is the best place to be at, for Christmas. Christmas is celebrated with a lot of enthusiasm in Goa. Goa is home to over 400 churches, big and small, and there's no better way to celebrate Christmas in Goa than attending a midnight mass. Followed by a treat on traditional Christmas dinner at a shack on the beach. You can watch fireworks lighting up the midnight sky and so on.

CHAPTER 3
History of India
(2500 BC-19th Century)

India's first major civilisation flourished for a
thousand years from around 2500 BC along
the Indus River valley. Its great cities were
Mohenjo-daro and Harappa (now in Pakistan),
ruled by priests and bearing the rudiments of
Hinduism, Aryan invaders swept south front
central Asia between 1500 and 200 BC and

controlled northern India, pushing the original Dravidian inhabitants to south.

The invaders brought their own Gods, cattle-raising and meat-eating traditions, but were absorbed to such a degree that by the 8th century BC, the priestly caste had reasserted its supremacy. This became consolidated in the caste system, a hierarchy maintained by strict rules that secured the position of the Brahmin priests. Buddhism arose around 500 BC, condemning caste; it drove a radical swathe through Hinduism in the 3rd century BC when it was embraced by the Mauryan Emperor Ashoka, who controlled huge tracts of India.

A number of empires, including the Gupta, rose and fell in the north after the collapse of the Mauryas. Hinduism underwent a revival from 40 to 600 AD and Buddhism began to decline. The north of India broke into a number of separate Hindu kingdoms after the Huns invasion; it was not really unified again until the coming of the Muslims. The far south, whose prosperity was based on trading links with the Egyptians, Romans and South-East Asia, was unaffected by the turmoil in the north and Hinduism's hold on the region was never threatened.

In 1192, Muslims arrived from the Middle East. Within 20 years the entire Ganges basin was under Muslim control, though Islam failed to penetrate the south. Two great kingdoms developed in what is now known as the State of Karnataka: One was the mighty Hindu kingdom of Vijayanagar and the other fragmented Bahmani Muslim kingdom.

Mughal emperors marched into the Punjab from Afghanistan, defeated the Sultan of Delhi in 1525 and ushered in another artistic golden age. The Maratha Empire grew during the 17th century and gradually took over most of the Mughals' domain. The Marathas consolidated control of central India until they fell to the last great imperial power, The British.

The British were not, however, the only European power in India: the Portuguese had controlled Goa since 1510 and the French,

Danes and Dutch also had trading posts. By 1803, when the British overwhelmed the Marathas, most of the country was under the control of the British East India Company, which had established its trading post at Surat in Gujarat in 1612.

The company treated India as a place to make money and its culture, beliefs and religions were left strictly alone. Britain expanded iron and coal mining, developed tea, coffee and cotton plantations and began construction of India's vast rail network. They encouraged absentee landlords because they eased the burden of administration and tax collection, creating an impoverished landless peasantry - a problem which is still chronic in Bihar and West Bengal. The Mutiny in northern India in 1857 led to the demise of the East India Company and administration of the country was handed over to the British Government.

CHAPTER 4
History of India
(1901- Till date)

Opposition to the British rule began in earnest at the turn of the 20th century. The 'Indian National Congress' which had been established to give India a degree of self-rule now began to push for the real thing. In 1915, Mahatma Gandhi returned from South Africa, where he had practised as a lawyer and turned his abilities to independence, adopting a policy of passive resistance or Satyagraha.

World War II dealt a deathblow to colonialism and Indian independence became inevitable. Within India, however, the large Muslim minority realized that an independent India would be Hindu-dominated. Communalism grew, with the Muslim League, led by Muhammad Ali Jinnah, speaking for the overwhelming majority of Muslims and the Congress Party, led by Jawaharlal Nehru, representing the Hindu population. The bid for a separate Muslim nation was the biggest stumbling block to Britain granting independence.

Faced with a political stand-off and rising tension, Viceroy Mountbatten reluctantly decided to divide the country and set a rapid timetable for independence. Unfortunately, the two overwhelmingly Muslim regions were on opposite sides of the country - meaning the new nation of Pakistan was divided by a hostile India. When the border line dividing Pakistan and India was announced, the greatest exodus in human history took place as Muslims moved to Pakistan and Hindus and Sikhs relocated to India. Over 10 million people changed sides and even the most conservative estimates calculate that 250,000 people were killed. On 30 January 1948, Gandhiji, deeply disheartened by partition and the subsequent bloodshed, was assassinated by a Hindu fanatic.

Following the trauma of Partition, India's first Prime Minister Jawaharlal Nehru championed a secular constitution, socialist central planning and a strict policy of non-alignment. India elected to join the Commonwealth, but also increased ties with the USSR - partly because of conflicts with China and partly because of US support for archenemy Pakistan, which was particularly hostile to India because of its claim on Muslim-dominated Kashmir. There were clashes with Pakistan in 1965 and 1971.

India's next Prime Minister of stature was Nehru's daughter Indira Gandhi, who was elected in 1966. She is still held in high esteem, but is remembered by some for meddling with India's democratic foundations by declaring a state of emergency in 1975. Mrs. Gandhi was assassinated by her Sikh bodyguards in 1984 as a reprisal for using the Indian Army to flush out armed Sikh radicals from the Golden Temple in Amritsar. The Gandhi's dynastic grip on Indian politics continued when her son, Rajiv Gandhi was swept into power.

Rajiv brought new and pragmatic policies to the country. Foreign investment and the use of modern technology were encouraged, import restrictions were eased and many new industries were set-up. These measures projected India into the 1990s and out of isolationism, but did little to stimulate India's mammoth rural sector. Rajiv Gandhi was assassinated on an election tour by a supporter of Sri Lanka's Tamil Tigers.

The dangers of communalism in India were clearly displayed in 1992, when a Hindu mob stormed and destroyed a mosque built on the site of Lord Rama's birth place Ayodhya. The Hindu nationalist, Bharatiya Janata Party (BJP) has been keen to exploit such opportunities and has led several disparate coalitions to power in recent years. Despite the dangers of playing communalist politics, the BJP's traditionalist Hindu stance attracted voters concerned about retaining traditional values during the sudden onslaught of modern global influences.

In 1998, India tested its first nuclear weapons. Despite international outrage, the nuclear tests were met with widespread jubilation in India and caused a groundswell of support for the BJP.

But by April 1999, Prime Minister Atal Bihari Vajpayee had lost majority support in parliament and was forced into a vote of confidence, which he lost by one vote. Sonia Gandhi, Rajiv Gandhi's widow, was expected to lead the Congress Party to victory after its three years in the political wilderness, but she was unable to secure a coalition and India was forced to the polls for the third time in as many years. The BJP was returned to government but with a significant decrease in support.

CHAPTER 5
Culture: Religion

Religion seeps into every facet of Indian life. Despite being a secular democracy, India is one of the few countries on earth in which the social and religious structures that define the nation's identity remain intact and have continued to do so for at least 4000 years despite invasions, persecution, European colonialism and political upheaval. Change is inevitably taking place as modern technology reaches ahead and further into the fabric of society but essentially rural India remains much the same as it has been for thousands of years. So resilient are its social and religious institutions that it has absorbed, ignored or thrown off all attempts to radically change or destroy them.

India's major religion, Hinduism, is practised by approximately 80% of the population. In terms of the number of adherents, it is the largest religion in Asia and one of the world's oldest extant faiths. Hinduism has a vast pantheon of Gods, a number of holy books and postulates that everyone goes through a series of births or reincarnations that eventually lead to spiritual salvation. With each birth, you can move closer to or further from eventual enlightenment; the deciding factor is your Karma. The Hindu religion has three basic practices. They are puja or worship, the cremation of the dead and the rules and regulations of the caste system. Hinduism is not a proselytising religion since you cannot be converted: You're either born a Hindu or you're not.

Buddhism was founded in northern India in about 500 BC, spread rapidly when emperor Ashoka embraced it, but was gradually reabsorbed into Hinduism. Today Hindus regard the Buddha as another incarnation of the Hindu God Vishnu. There are now only 6.6 million Buddhists in India, but important Buddhist sites in northern India, such as Bodhgaya, Sarnath (near Varanasi) and Kushinagar (near Gorakhpur) remain important sites of pilgrimage. The Jain religion also began into life as an attempt to reform Brahminical Hinduism. It emerged at the same time as Buddhism and for many of the same principles & reasons. The Jains are now only about 4.5 million in numbers and are found predominantly in the west and south-west of India. The religion has never found adherents outside India. Jains believe that the universe is infinite and was not created by a deity. They also believe in reincarnation and eventual spiritual salvation by following the path of the Jain prophets.

There are more than 100 million Muslims in India, making it one of the largest Muslim nations on earth. Islam is the dominant religion in the neighbouring countries of Pakistan and Bangladesh. In India, Jammu & Kashmir bears a Muslim majority . Muslim influence in India is particularly strong in the fields of architecture, art and food. The Sikhs in India number to 18 million and are pre-dominantly located in Punjab. The religion was originally intended to bring together the best of Hinduism and Islam. Its basic tenets are similar to those of Hinduism with the important modification that the Sikhs are opposed to caste distinctions. The holiest shrine of the Sikh religion is the Golden Temple in Amritsar.

CHAPTER 6
Culture: Dialects

India is as close as the world comes to 'Babel'. There's no 'Indian' language per se, which is partly why English is still widely spoken almost half a century after the British left India. Eighteen languages are officially recognised by the constitution, but over 1600 minor languages and dialects were listed in the 1991 census. Language is a heavily politicised issue, not least because many state boundaries have been drawn on linguistic lines. Major efforts have been made to promote Hindi as the national language and to gradually phase out English. A stumbling block to this plan is that while Hindi is the pre-dominant language in the north, it bears little relation to the Dravidian languages of the south. In the south, very few people speak Hindi. The Indian upper class clings to English as the shared language of the educated elite, championing it as both a badge of their status and as a passport to the world of international business. In truth, only about 3% of Indians have a firm grasp of the language.

Indian art is basically religious in its themes and developments and its appreciation requires at least some background knowledge of the country's faiths. The highlights include classical Indian dance, Hindu temple architecture and sculpture the military and urban architecture of the Mughals, miniature painting and mesmeric Indian music. Indians love the cinema and the Indian film industry, centred in Mumbai, is one of the largest and most glamorous in the world. The vast proportions of films produced are gaudy melodramas based on three vital ingredients: romance, violence and music. You'll know what to expect from the fantastically hand-painted cinema billboards that dominate many streets. Imagine Rambo crossed with The Sound of Music and a Cecil B De Mille biblical epic and you're halfway there. It's cheap operatic escapism, extremely harsh on the ears and should not be missed.

Contrary to popular belief, not all Hindus are officially vegetarians. Although you'll find vegetarians everywhere, strict vegetarianism is most prevalent in the south (which has not been influenced by meat-eating Aryans and Muslims) and in the Gujarati community. There are considerable regional variations from north to south, partly because of climatic conditions and partly because of historical influences. In the north, much more meat is eaten and the cuisine is often 'Mughal style', which bears a closer relationship to food of the Middle East and Central Asia. The emphasis is more on spices and less on chilli; grains and breads are more popular than rice. In the south, more rice is eaten, there is more vegetarian food and the curries tend to be hotter. Another feature of southern vegetarian food is that you do not use cutleries for eating; just scoop the food up with your fingers - though not with those of your left hand.

CHAPTER 7
Environment of India

India is a large, triangular-shaped country in southern Asia, buttressed by the long sweep of the Himalaya in the north and protruding into the Indian Ocean in the south. It's bordered by Pakistan to the north-west, China, Nepal and Bhutan to the north and Bangladesh and Myanmar to the east. Sri Lanka is the teardrop-shaped island hanging off India's southern tip. India covers a land area of some 3,287,000 sq km

(1,281,930sq mi), though disputed borders with Pakistan and China make this figure somewhat arbitrary. It is the seventh largest country in the world.

Northern India contains the snow-bound peaks, deep valleys of the Himalaya and the vast Gangetic Plain, which separates the Himalayan region from the southern peninsula and stretches from the Arabian Sea to the Bay of Bengal. South of the plains, the land rises up into a triangular-shaped plateau known as the Deccan, which ranges in altitude from 300 m (985ft) to 900 m (2950ft). The plateau is bordered by the Eastern and Western Ghats, ranges of hills which run parallel to India's eastern and western coasts and separate the fertile coastal strips from the interior.

Wildlife in India is often purported to have enjoyed a privileged and protected position, thanks to the religious ideals and sentiments of Hindus, Jains and Buddhists, but much of this tradition has been lost. Extensive hunting by the British and the Indian rajas, large-scale clearing of forests for agriculture, poaching, pesticides and the ever-increasing population have had disastrous effects on India's environment. Only around 10 per cent of the country still has forest cover and only 4 percent is protected within national parks and reserves. In the past few decades, the Government has taken serious steps to improve environmental management and has established over 350 parks, sanctuaries and reserves.

The highlights of India's fauna are its lions, tigers, leopards, panthers, elephants and rhinoceroses, but the country is also home to a rich variety of deer and antelope, wild buffaloes, massive Indian bisons, shaggy sloth bears, striped hyenas, wild pigs, jackals and Indian wild dogs. Monkeys include rhesus macaques, bonnet macaques and long-tailed common langurs. The reptilian world boasts magnificent king cobras, pythons, crocodiles, large freshwater tortoises and monitor lizards, while the diverse birdlife includes large hornbills, serpent eagles and fishing owls, as well as the elegant national bird, the peacock.

Climate varies greatly, from the arid deserts of Rajasthan to the cool highlands of Assam, allegedly the wettest place on earth. But basically India has a three-season year - the hot, the wet and the cool. The heat starts to build up on the northern plains around February and by April it becomes unbearable. The first signs of the monsoon appear in May with high humidity, short rainstorms and violent electrical storms. The monsoon rains begin around June in the extreme south and sweep north to cover the whole country by early July. The monsoon doesn't really cool things off, but it's a great relief - especially to farmers. The main monsoon comes from the south-west, but the south-eastern coast is affected by the short and surprisingly wet north-eastern monsoon, which brings rain from mid-October to the end of December. The main monsoon ends around October and India's northern cities become chilled at night in December. In the far south, where it never gets cool, the temperatures are comfortably warm rather than hot.

CHAPTER 8
Flag, Emblem and
Preamble of India

The National flag is a horizontal tricolour of deep saffron (kesari) at the top, white in the middle and dark green at the bottom in equal proportion.

The ratio of width of the flag to its length is two to three. In the centre of the white band is a navy blue wheel which represents the chakra.

Its design is that of the wheel which appears on the abacus of the Sarnath, the Lion Capital of Ashoka. Its diameter approximates to the width of the white band and it has 24 spokes.

The design of the national flag was adopted by the Constituent Assembly of India on 22 July, 1947. Its use and display are regulated by the Indian Flag Code.

The Emblem

The State emblem is an adaptation from the Sarnath Lion Capital of Ashoka. In the original, there are four lions, standing back to back, mounted on an abacus with a frieze carrying sculptures in high relief of an elephant, a galloping horse, a bull and a lion separated by intervening 24 spoked wheels over a bell-shaped lotus. Carved out of a single block of polished sandstone, the capital is crowned by the Wheel of the Law (Dharma Chakra).

In the State emblem, adopted by the Government of India on 26 January 1950, only three lions are visible, the fourth being hidden from view. The wheel appears in relief in the centre of the abacus with a bull on right and a horse on left and the outlines of other wheels on extreme right and left. The bell-shaped lotus has been omitted. The words Satyameva Jayate from Mundaka Upanishad, meaning Truth Alone Triumphs', are inscribed below the abacus in Devanagari script.

Preamble of India

Preamble

PREAMBLE

WE THE PEOPLE OF INDIA having solemnly resolved to constitute India into a SOVEREIGN SOCIALIST SECULAR DEMOCRATIC REPUBLIC and to secure to all it's citizen

JUSTICE, social, economic and political
LIBERTY of thought, expression, belief, faith and worship
EQUALITY of status and of opportunity
and to promote among them all.
FRATERNITY assuring the dignity of individual and the unity and integrity of the nation.

IN OUR CONSTITUENT ASSEMBLY the twenty-sixth day of November, 1949, do, HEREBY ADOPT, ENACT AND GIVE TO OURSELVES THIS CONSTITUTION

WE, THE PEOPLE OF INDIA, having solemnly resolved to constitute India into a [SOVEREIGN SOCIALIST SECULAR DEMOCRATIC REPUBLIC] and to secure to all its citizens:

JUSTICE, social, economic and political;

LIBERTY of thought, expression, belief, faith and worship; EQUALITY of status and of opportunity; and to promote among them all

FRATERNITY assuring the dignity of the individual and the unity and integrity of the Nation.

IN OUR CONSTITUENT ASSEMBLY this twenty-sixth day of November, 1949, do HEREBY ADOPT, ENACT AND GIVE TO OURSELVES THIS CONSTITUTION

CHAPTER 9
The National Anthem and Song of India

The National Anthem

The song 'Jana-gana-mana', composed originally in Bengali by India's first Nobel laureate Rabindranath Tagore on December 11, 1911, was adopted in its Hindi version by the Constituent Assembly as the National Anthem of India on 24 January 1950. It was first sung on 27 December 1911 at the Calcutta Session of the Indian National Congress. The complete song consists of five stanzas. The first stanza contains the full version of the National Anthem :

Jana-gana-mana-adhinayaka, jaya he
Bharata-bhagya-vidhata.
Punjab-Sindh-Gujarat-Maratha

Dravida-Utkala-Banga
Vindhya-Himachala-Yamuna-Ganga
Uchchala-Jaladhi-taranga.
Tava shubha name jage,
Tava shubha asisa mage,
Gahe tava jaya gatha,
Jana-gana-mangala-dayaka jaya he
Bharata-bhagya-vidhata.
Jaya he, jaya he, jaya he,
Jaya jaya jaya, jaya he!

The following is Tagore's English rendering of the anthem:

Thou art the ruler of the minds of all people,
Dispenser of India's destiny.
Thy name rouses the hearts of Punjab, Sind,
Gujarat and Maratha,
Of the Dravida and Orissa and Bengal;
It echoes in the hills of the Vindyas and Himalayas,
Mingles in the music of Yamuna and Ganga
And is chanted by the waves of the Indian Sea.
They pray for thy blessings and sing thy praise.
The salvation of all people is in thy hand,

Thou dispenser of India's destiny.
Victory, victory, victory to thee.

The National Song

The song 'Vande Mataram', composed in Sanskrit by Bankim Chandra Chattopadhyay, was a source of inspiration to the people of India in their struggle for freedom. It shares equal status with that of Jana-gana-mana. The first political occasion when 'Vande Mataram' was sung, was in 1896 session of the Indian National Congress. The following is the text of its first stanza:

Vande Mataram!
Sujalam, suphalam, malayaja shitalam,
Sasyashyamalam, Mataram!
Shubhrajyothsna pulakitayaminim,
Pullakusumita drumadala shobhinim,
Suhasinim sumadhura bhashinim,
Sukhadam varadam, Mataram!

The English translation of the stanza rendered by Sri Aurobindo Ghose in prose is :

I bow to thee, Mother,
richly-watered, richly-fruited,

cool with the winds of the south,

dark with the crops of the harvests,

The Mother!

Her nights rejoicing in the glory of the moonlight,

her lands clothed beautifully with her trees in flowering bloom,

sweet of laughter, sweet of speech,

The Mother, giver of boons, giver of bliss.

CHAPTER 10
The National Symbols of India

	Month	Length	Start date (Gregorian)
1	Chaitra	30/31	March 22*
2	Vaishākh	31	April 21
3	Jyaishtha	31	May 22
4	Āshādha	31	June 22
5	Shrāvana	31	July 23
6	Bhādrapad	31	August 23
7	Āshwin	30	September 23
8	Kārtik	30	October 23
9	Mārgashīrsha (Agrahayana)	30	November 22
10	Paush	30	December 22
11	Māgh	30	January 21
12	Phālgun	30	February 20

The National Calendar

The national calendar based on the Saka Era with Chaitra as its first month and a normal year of 365 days was adopted from 22 March 1957 alongwith the Gregorian calendar for the following official purposes: (i) Gazette of India, (ii) news broadcast by All India Radio,

(iii) calendars issued by the Government of India and (iv) Government communications addressed to the members of the public.

Dates of the national calendar have a permanent correspondence with dates of the Gregorian calendar: Chaitra the first month of the year begins on 22 March and however during leap year the starting day of Chaitra falls on 21 March.

The National Animal

The magnificent tiger, Panthera tigris (Linnaeus), is the largest cat species recognized by their pattern of dark horizontal stripes on thick yellow coat of fur. The combination of grace, strength, agility and enormous power has earned the tiger its pride of place as the national animal of India. Out of eight races of the species known, the Indian race, the Royal Bengal Tiger, is found throughout the country except in the north- western region. They are also found in the neighbouring countries, Nepal, Bhutan and Bangladesh. To check the dwindling population of tigers in India, 'Project Tiger' was launched in April 1973. So far, 25 tiger reserves have been established in the country under this project, covering an area of 33,875 sq km.

The National Bird

The Indian peacock, Pavo cristatus (Linnaeus), the National Bird of India, is a colourful, swan-sized bird, with a fan-shaped crest of feathers, a white patch under the eye and a long, slender neck.

The male of the species is more colourful than the female, with a glistening blue breast and neck and a spectacular bronze-green tail of around 200 elongated feathers. The female is brownish, slightly smaller than the male and lacks the tail. The elaborate courtship dance of the male, fanning out the tail and preening its feathers, is a gorgeous sight.

The peacock is widely found in the Indian subcontinent from the south and east of the Indus river, Jammu and Kashmir, east Assam, south Mizoram and the whole of the Indian peninsula. The Peacock enjoys protection from the people as it is never molested for religious and sentimental reasons. It is fully protected under the Indian Wildlife (Protection) Act, 1972.

The National Flower

Lotus (Nelumbo Nucifera Gaertn) is the National Flower of India. It is a sacred flower and occupies a unique position in the art and mythology of ancient India and has been an auspicious symbol of Indian culture since time immemorial.

CHAPTER 11
States and Languages of India

States of India

It has been said that the states of India are more diverse than the countries in Europe. From the largest to the smallest, each has a unique history and culture, dress, festivals and way of celebrating them.

National Capital Territory - Delhi

Capital of India-New Delhi

STATES	CAPITALS
Andhra Pradesh	Hyderabad
Arunachal Pradesh	Itanagar
Assam	Dispur
Bihar	Patna
Chhattisgarh	Raipur
Goa	Panaji

Gujarat	Gandhinagar
Haryana	Chandigarh
Himachal Pradesh	Shimla
Jammu and Kashmir	Srinagar (Summer capital) Jammu (Winter capital)
Jharkhand	Ranchi
Karnataka	Bangalore
Kerala	Thiruvananthapuram
Madhya Pradesh	Bhopal
Maharashtra	Mumbai
Manipur	Imphal
Meghalaya	Shillong
Mizoram	Aizawl
Nagaland	Kohima
Odisha	Bhubaneshwar
Punjab	Chandigarh
Rajasthan	Jaipur
Sikkim	Gangtok
Tamil Nadu	Chennai
Telangana	Hyderabad
Tripura	Agartala

Uttar Pradesh	Lucknow
Uttaranchal	Dehradun
West Bengal	Kolkata

Union Territories	**Headquarters**
Andaman and Nicobar Islands	Port Blair
Chandigarh	Chandigarh
Dadra and Nagar Haveli	Silvassa
Daman and Diu	Daman
Lakshadweep	Kavaratti
Puducherry	Pondicherry
Delhi	New Delhi

Languages of India

Currently, there are around 22 languages recognised by the Indian Constitution. These languages are

1. Assamese
2. Bengali
3. Bodo
4. Dogri
5. Gujarati

6. Hindi
7. Kannada
8. Kashmiri
9. Konkani
10. Maithili
11. Malayalam
12. Manipuri
13. Marathi
14. Nepali
15. Odia
16. Punjabi
17. Sanskrit
18. Santhali
19. Sindhi
20. Tamil
21. Telugu
22. Urdu

Hindi is the official and main link language of India. Its homeland is mainly in the north of India, but it is spoken and widely understood in all urban centers of India. It is written in the Devanagri script, which is phonetic and, unlike English, is pronounced as it is written. Hindi is a direct descendant of Sanskrit through Prakrit and Apabhramsha. It has been influenced and enriched by Dravidian, Turkish, Farsi, Arabic, Portuguese and English. It is a very expressive language. In poetry and songs, it can convey emotions using simple and gentle words. It can also be used for exact and rational reasoning.

CHAPTER 12
Geography of India

India is the seventh largest country in the world with a total land area of 3.3 million square kilometers. It is 2933 kms wide and the 3214 kms long. The Indian sub-continent is unique from the rest of Asia. In the North are the towering Himalayas which slope out into the great Indo-Gangetic plains. In Central India, the Vindhya ranges separate the Deccan Peninsula from the northern plains. On the east coast of the country is the Bay of Bengal, while on the west coast is the Arabian Sea. The southern-most tip of the country projects into the Indian Ocean.

Deccan plateau

The Deccan plateau is the oldest portion of India and was part of the single land mass comprising South America, Africa, Australia and Antarctica. As the continents drifted apart, the moving Deccan plate collided with the Tibetan block of South Asia about 50 million years ago. Over the years, the persistent pressure of the Deccan drifting northwards created the Himalayan mountains, a process that is still continuing.

Indo-Gangetic plain

The Indo-Gangetic plain is formed by the basins of three great rivers, the Indus, the Ganges and the Brahmaputra. The other major rivers in the country are the Mahanadi, Godavari, Krishna, Narmada, Kaveri, Pennar, Tapti and Periyar - all of which have created deltas and flood-plains on India's east and west coast.

Varied geography

Apart from the mountains, plains and the seas, India has just about every geographical feature as well. In the West of the country lies the Thar desert in Rajasthan. A little south of it are the unique marshlands of Kutch, while on the east where the Ganges drains out into the sea is the world' s largest delta and a unique mangrove forest. Indian islands include the Andaman and Nicobar Islands in the Bay of Bengal and the Lakshadweep Islands in the Indian ocean. These unique features mean that the country has a wide variety of flora, fauna and a climate that ranges from tropical to arctic.

Climate

The climate of the country varies from region to region. The North enjoys cold climate in the-winter months between November and March. The coastal areas have a tropical, climate throughout the year, while the plains and most central and southern regions of the country are hot in the summer months of April and June. Most of the country has a vigorous monsoon, which lasts from July and October.

Located in the northern hemisphere, India shares its borders with Pakistan, Afghanistan, China, Nepal, Bhutan, Myanmar and Bangladesh. The rest of the land is surrounded by sea.

CHAPTER 13
Activities in the Country

The number of trekkers visiting the Indian Himalayas is small compared to those tramping the tracks in Nepal, so if you want to peacefully experience the world's greatest mountain range, try trekking in Himachal Pradesh or Uttar Pradesh. The trekking season runs roughly between April and November, but this varies widely and some routes are only open for a couple of months each year. India's main trekking centres are Lahaul, Spiti and the Kullu and Kangra valleys in Himachal Pradesh; north of Rishikesh in northern Uttar Pradesh; Darjeeling in West Bengal; Yuksam in Sikkim; and Leh in Ladakh.

The ski season runs from January to March and there are resorts at Narkanda in Himachal Pradesh and Auli in Uttar Pradesh. Facilities are rudimentary but that makes it all the more fun. There's usually one lift in working order and a place to hire gear. Apres-ski consists of chapmen and a nice cup of ginger tea.

India is not renowned for its beaches, but there are popular beach centres with acceptable swimming in Goa, just across the Karnataka border in Gokarna and at Kovalam in Kerala. There are also beaches at Diu and at Puri in Orissa. The Andaman & Nicobar Islands in the Bay of Bengal have good beaches and boast India's only diving and snorkelling opportunities.

Camel treks can be arranged in the deserts around Jaisalmer and Pushkar in Rajasthan. Treks last anywhere between few hours and few days. The best season is between October and February. If camel trekking leaves you feeling scorched and sore, try white-water rafting on the Indus. Trips can be organised in Leh.

CHAPTER 14
Religions and Languages of India

Religions

As the birth place of four major religion, that exist even today, India is rightfully known as the land of spirituality and philosophy. The most dominant religion in India today is Hinduism with almost 81% of the people being Hindus. One of the truly ancient religions of the world, Hinduism is believed to have developed nearly 5000 years ago.

Around 500 BC, two other religions made their mark in India: Buddhism and Jainism. Though today these two religions together account for not more than 1.2% of the population, their impact on Indian culture and sensibility is far in excess of that. Between them these three ancient religions -Hinduism, Buddhism and Jainism - moulded Indian philosophy and thinking. One comparatively new religion in India is Sikhism which was established in the 15th century. Today about 2% of Indians are Sikhs. There were other attempts to create new religions in India, though they did not always succeed, they add to the mystic lore and spiritual depth of the land. For example, the great Mughal emperor, Akbar, who reigned between 1556 and 1605, tried to establish a new religion, Din-I-Ilahi. . However, this movement never had much followers.

Alongwith the religions that developed in India, there are followers of non-Indian religions as well. Islam is the chosen faith of a hefty 14.29% of India's population. Christians account for more than 2% and Zoroastrians (Parsis) though a tiny minority, still make their presence felt. There are also a few thousand Jews in India.

Languages of India

India's official language is Hindi in the Devanagri script. It is the primary tongue of

30% of the people.

The States are free to decide their own regional languages for internal administration and education, so there are 22 official languages spoken throughout the country. Bengali, Telugu, Marathi, Tamil, Urdu, Gujarati, Malayalam, Kannada, Odia, Punjabi, Assamese, Kashmiri and Sindhi, are among the official languages which are also widely spoken. Sanskrit though an official language, is hardly ever used except in rituals and ceremonies.

While English enjoys an associate status, it is widely spoken and is one of the most important languages for national, political and commercial communication.

In all, there are 24 different languages, each spoken by a million or more persons; as well as millions of other languages and dialects.

CHAPTER 15
Main Attractions of India

Delhi

Your first impression of Delhi is unlikely to be a good one, particularly if it's also your first impression of India. You'll most likely notice the pollution, the crowds, the smell, the noise and the ceaseless hassles long before you notice the city's charms. But it's worth persevering as the history of this city is fascinating and it's all around you: the bazaars of Paharganj are a wonderful introduction to India's backpacker trail; the city's monuments are among the most architecturally striking in the country; and the food here is great.

Delhi is the capital of India and it's also the travel hub of northern India. It's an excellent base for visiting Agra and the Taj Mahal. Also the Rajasthani colour of Jaipur is less than five hours away. If you're heading north to the Himalayas or east to the Ghats of Varanasi, you'll probably pass through Delhi. So you might as well grit your teeth, hold your breath and dive on in.

Udaipur

The most romantic city in Rajasthan, built around the lovely Lake Pichola, has inevitably been dubbed the 'Venice of the East'. Founded in 1568 by Maharana Udai Singh, the city is a harmonious Indian blend of whitewashed buildings, marble palaces, lakeside gardens, temples and havelis (traditional mansions).

Lake Pichola is the city's centrepiece and it contains two delightful island palaces - Jagniwas and Jagmandir - they are the very definition of Rajput whimsy. The former is now an exquisite luxury hotel. The huge City Palace towers over the lake and is bedecked with balconies, towers and cupolas. It contains a museum, some fine gardens and several more luxury hotels. Other attractions in Udaipur include the gates to the old walled city and its lovely alleyways; the fine Indo-Aryanjagdish Temple, daring from the mid-17th century; and the lakeside Bagore ki Haveli, once a royal guesthouse, but now a cultural centre.

Despite the long list of sights and attractions, the real joy of Udaipur is finding a pleasant lakeside guesthouse, scrambling up to the roof and watching the activity at the Ghats, listening to the rhythmic 'thwomp!' as washerwomen thrash the life out of their laundry and sensing the gentle changes of light on the water as the slow days progress.

Indian Airlines has daily flights to Delhi, Jaipur, Mumbai and Aurangabad. Frequent state-owned buses run from Udaipur to other regional centres as well as to Delhi and Ahmedabad. If you want to take bus , choose the express, otherwise it will take forever to reach your destination. Lines into Udaipur are currently metre gauge only. They are scheduled to be converted to broad gauge, but nobody is really sure when this will happen. It's quicker in most cases to catch a bus. Taxis can take you to regional areas, but practise your negotiation skills and haggle down the price a bit before you jump in.

CHAPTER 16
Mumbai and Jaipur

Mumbai

Mumbai is the glamour of Bollywood cinema, Cricket on the maidans (sports ground) on weekends, Bhelpuri on the beach at Chowpatty and red double-decker buses. It is also the infamous cages of the red-light district, Asia's largest slums, communalist politics and powerful mafia dons. This tug of war for the city's soul is played out against a Victorian townscape more reminiscent of a prosperous 19th century English industrial city than anything you'd expect to find on the edge of the Arabian Sea.

Jaipur

The capital of Rajasthan is popularly known as the 'Pink City' because of the ochre-pink hue of its old buildings and crenellated city walls. The Rajputs considered pink to be a colour associated with hospitality and are reputed to have daubed the city in preparation for the visit of Britain's Prince Alfred in 1853. This tradition and Jaipur's welcoming relaxed air continue to this day.

Jaipur owes its name, its foundation and its careful planning to the great warrior-astronomer Maharaja Jai Singh II (1699-1744), who took advantage of declining Mughal power to move his somewhat cramped hillside fortress at nearby Amber to a new site on the plains in 1727. He laid out the city's surrounding walls and its six rectangular blocks with the help of Shilpa-Shastra, an ancient Hindu treatise on architecture.

Today Jaipur is a city of broad avenues and remarkable architectural harmony, built on a dry lake bed surrounded by barren hills. It's an extremely colourful city and, in the evening light, it radiates a magical warm glow. The city now has 1.5 million inhabitants and has sprawled beyond its original fortified confines, but most of its attractions are compactly located in the walled 'Pink City' in the north-east of the city. All seven gates into the old city remain, one of which leads into Johari Bazaar - the famous jewellers' market.

The most obvious landmark in the old city is the Iswari Minar Swarga Sul (the Minaret Piercing Heaven) which was built to overlook the city, but the most striking sight is the stunning artistry of the five-storey facade of the Hawa Mahal or Palace of the Winds. The palace was built in 1799 to enable ladies of the royal household to watch street life and processions and is part of the City Palace complex which forms the heart of the old city.

Numerous international airlines are based in Jaipur Towers, while for domestic flights it's easier to book through any of the big travel agents. Daily flights to Delhi are available and most continue on to Mumbai via Jodhpur, Udaipur and Aurangabad. The Rajasthan State Transport System covers Rajasthan's major cities, as do the privately owned deluxe services. Most of these places can also be reached by train.

CHAPTER 17
Kolkata

The capital of West Bengal sprawls shapelessly along the eastern bank of the Hooghly River. Once the glorious capital of British India, its urban horror story of squalor and starvation only began with partition and a resulting massive influx of refugees. This plucky city, however, is keen to promote itself as the 'City of Joy' and given half a chance, it reveals itself to be one of the country's most fascinating congenial cities, the intellectual capital of the nation and a thriving political and arts arena.

Some welcome space is provided by the Maidan, an enormous open expanse used by Kolkatans for recreation, cricket and football matches, political assemblies, yoga sessions and grazing flocks. At the southern end of the Maidan stands the huge white-marble Victoria Memorial, fronted by a statue of a frumpy Queen Victoria, which holds an extensive collection of British-Indian historical objects.

Kolkata's administrative centre is B.B.D. Bagh (Dalhousie Square). The square holds both the whimsical and the brutal: On one side is the Writers' Building where 'writers' (a quaint euphemism for clerks) beaver away in the Kafkaesque labyrinth of corridors and vast chambers while quintuplicate forms and carbon copies pile up along the walls; on the other side is the GPO which was built on the site of the legendary 'Black Hole of Kolkata'.

According to legend, when Siva's wife's corpse was cut up, one of her fingers fell at the site of what is now the Kali Temple at Kalighat and it remains one of the important pilgrimages of India. The city's other attractions include: the excellent Indian Museum, the largest and probably the best museum in the country, the Botanical Gardens, home to a 200-year-old banyan tree, claimed to have the second-largest canopy in the world (the largest is in Andhra Pradesh); and the iconic cantilevered Howrah Bridge, considered to be the busiest bridge in the world.

Budget accommodation, low cost eateries and bars are thick on the ground in Chowringhee, south of the Howrah Bridge. Sudder Street, off Chowringhee Road, is the focal point for budget travellers. There are also lots of cinemas in this area, screening Kolkatan art house fare, new release Hollywood movies and their Hollywood cousins.

Kolkata is on the international loop and you can sometimes pick up cut price tickets at the airlines offices around Chowringhee. Kolkata's Indian Airlines offers frequent domestic flights to major Indian destinations including Delhi, Bangalore, Chennai, Mumbai and Lucknow. Generally speaking, it's better to travel by train rather than bus but if it's a bus you're after, you'll be looking at catching the dubiously named 'Rocket Service' from the Esplanade bus stand. For outbound trains, go to either Howrah station on the west bank of the Hooghly river which handles trains going to the city or Sealdah station on the opposite side which takes you in the direction of Darjeeling and other northern regions.

CHAPTER 18
Goa and Agra

Goa

Goa comes burdened with a history of louche living because there's so much more to it than sun, sand and psychedelia. The allure of Goa is that it remains quite distinct from the rest of India and is small enough to be grasped and explored in a way that other Indian states are not. It's not just the familiar remnants of European colonialism or the picture-book exoticism that make it seem so accessible, it's the prevalence of Roman Catholicism and a form of social and political progressiveness that Westerners feel they can relate to. Although Hindus make up two-thirds of the population, the people of Goa are more liberal-minded than imperviously devout, in a way that is unmatched elsewhere in India.

Agra

The Taj Mahal, described as the most extravagant monument ever built for love, has become the de facto tourist emblem of India. This poignant Mughal mausoleum was constructed by Emperor Shah Jahan in memory of his second wife Mumtaz Mahal, whose death in childbirth in 1631 left the emperor so heartbroken that his hair is said to have turned grey overnight. Construction of the Taj Mahal began in the same year and was completed during the year 1653.

The emperor's hair may have gone shabby but his eye for detail apparently remained acute: the near-perfection of the Taj's architecture does not diminish upon closer inspection; it merely comes into sharper focus. Semiprecious stones were laid into the marble in elaborate designs through a process called Pietra Dura. If you're planning to check out this marvel, don't forget that it's closed on Friday to all non-Muslims.

The city's other major attraction is the massive red sandstone Agra Fort, on the bank of the Yamuna River. The auricular fort's Colossal I double walls rise over 20m (65ft) in height and measure 2.5 km (1.55mi) in circumference. They are encircled by a fetid moat and contain a maze of superb halls, mosques, chambers and gardens which form a small city within a city. Unfortunately not all buildings are open to visitors, including the white marble Pearl Mosque, regarded by some as the most beautiful mosque in India.

Other worthwhile Mughal gems include the Itimad-ud-daulah, many of whose design elements were used in the construction of the Taj and Akbar's Mausoleum at Sikandra which blends Islamic, Hindu, Buddhist, Jain and Christian motifs, much like the syncretic religious philosophy Akbar developed and attempted to do. Agra is near enough to Delhi - 200 km (125mi) easy to be done as a day trip. It's on the major tourism circuit so you can take your pick of transport; plane, bus or train.

CHAPTER 19
Varanasi

For over 2000 years, Varanasi, the 'Eternal City', has been the religious capital of India. Built on the banks of the sacred Ganges, it is said to combine the virtues of all other places of pilgrimage and anyone who ends their days here, regardless of creed and however great their misdeeds, is transported straight to heaven. The easternmost city in Uttar Pradesh, Varanasi is an important seat of learning and is the home of novelists, philosophers and grammarians. This has been reflected in its role in the development of Hindi - the closest thing to a national language in India.

Varanasi has over 100 bathing and burning Ghats but the Manikarnika Ghat is the most sacred of them all. This is the main burning ghat and one of the most auspicious places that a Hindu can be cremated. Corpses are handled by outcasts known as Chandal and they are carried through the alleyways of the old city to the holy Ganges on a bamboo stretcher swathed in cloth. You'll see huge piles of firewood stacked along the top of the ghat, each log carefully weighed on giant scales so that the price of cremation can be calculated. There are no problems watching cremations, since at Manikarnika death is simply business as usual, but leave your camera at your hotel.

The best ghat to hang out at and absorb the riverside activity is Dasaswamedh Ghat. Here you'll find a dense concentration of people who come to the edge of the Ganges not only for a ritual bath, but to do yoga, offer blessings, buy paan, sell flowers, get a massage, play cricket, have a swim, get a shave and do their karma good by giving money to beggars. It's also the best place to arrange a boat trip since there's plenty of competition among boatmen.

Apart from the many ghats lining the river, the city's other highlights include the Golden Temple, built in a roofed quadrangle with stunning gilded towers; shopping at markets famous for their ornamental brasswork, lacquered toys, shawls, silks and sitars (yes, Ravi Shankar does live here); losing yourself in the impossibly narrow labyrinthine alleyways which snake back from the ghats; visiting the nearby Buddhist centre of Sarnath; and taking the compulsory dawn river trip slowly down the Ganges.

Varanasi is on the major tourist loop, about 580km (360mi) east of Agra and 780km (485mi) southeast of Delhi and can be reached by plane, bus or train.

CHAPTER 20
Shimla

The 'Summer Capital' of British India sprawls along a crescent-shaped ridge at an altitude of over 2100m (6890ft) in southern Himachal Pradesh. This was the most important hill station in India before Independence and the social life here in the summer months, when the British came to escape the torrid heat of the plains was legendary - balls, bridge parties and parades went hand in hand with gossip, intrigue and romance. Today, the officers, administrators and lah-di-dah ladies of the Raj have been replaced by throngs of holidaymakers, but echoes of Shimla's British past remain strong. The famous main-street, The Mall Street, still runs along the crest of the ridge and is lined with stately English-looking houses. Christ Church, Gorton Castle and the fortress-like former Viceregal Lodge reinforce the English flavour.

When you've done the obligatory stroll along The Mall dreaming of Kipling, Burton and Merchant-Ivory, its worth exploring the narrow streets which fall steeply away from the ridge to colourful local bazaars. There's also an interesting walk to Jakhu Temple, dedicated to the monkey god Hanuman. It's located near the highest point of the ridge and offers fine views of the town, surrounding valley and snow-capped peaks. Other scenic spots nearby include the 70m (230ft) high Chadwick Falls, the picnic spot of Prospect Hill and Wildflower Hall - the site of the former mansion of Lord 'Your-Country-Needs-You' Kitchener. The ski resort of Kufri is just 15km (10m) east, although snowfalls have been so paltry recently that there are plans to suspend tourist operations. If there is snow, the slopes are suitable for beginners and anyone with a decent plastic bag and a thick pair of trousers. Snow is most likely between January and February.

Shimla is not as well connected by air as other destinations in the Himalayas although, there are a couple of companies that will fly you out. The lack of air power is more than compensated by the number of trains and buses. Three types of bus - public, private and those from the Himachal Pradesh Tourist Development Company (HPTDC) - connect Shimla to Delhi and they run pretty much every day. Shimla's so-called toy train is still big enough to get you to Kalka in the north, after which you can change to the relatively large and comfortable New Delhi Queen which runs on down into New Delhi.

CHAPTER 21
Mysore and Kochi

Mysore

This charming, easy-going city has long been a favourite with travellers since it's of a manageable size, enjoys a good climate and has chosen to retain and promote its heritage rather than replace it. The city is famous for its silk and is also a thriving sandalwood and incense centre, though don't expect the air to be any more fragrant than the next town.

Until Independence, Mysore was the seat of the maharajas of Mysore, a princely state covering about a third of present-day Karnataka. The Maharaja's Indo-Saracenic Palace is the town's major attraction, with its kaleidoscope of stained glass, ornate mirrors, carved mahogany ceilings, solid silver doors and outrageously gaudy colours.

The Devaraja Fruit & Vegetable Market, in the heart of the town, is one of the most colourful markets in India. The other major attraction is the 1000-step climb up nearby Chamundi Hill, which is topped by the huge Chamundeswari temple. The stairway is guarded by the famous 5m (16ft) high Nandi (Siva's bull) carved out of solid rock. The 10-day Dussehra Festival in early October culminates in a spectacular procession of richly caparisoned elephants, liveried retainers, cavalry, brass bands and flower-bedecked images of Hindu deities.

There are no flights to Mysore, leaving the bus and train as the only options. Every 15 minutes a bus to Bangalore hurtles out of the starting blocks like a bat out of hell, as do a number of other services going to regional areas including the Bandipur National Park. A number of private buses will take you to a far more sedate place as Mumbai, Goa, Chennai and Hyderabad. There are rarely long queues to book a fare at Mysore station and there are four daily express trains to Bangalore, plus the air-con high-speed Shatabdi Express which departs at 2.10 pm daily except Tuesday. The Shatabdi continues on to Chennai.

Kochi (Cochin)

The port city of Kochi is located on a cluster of islands and narrow peninsulas. The older parts of the city are an unlikely blend of medieval Portugal, Holland and an English country villa grafted onto the tropical Malabar Coast. Down neat the waterfront you can see St. Francis Church, India's oldest; a 450-year-old Portuguese palace; Chinese fishing nets strung out past Fort Cochin; and a synagogue dating back to the mid-16th century. Ferries scuttle back and forth between the various parts of Kochi and dolphins can often be seen in the harbour. Most of the historical sites are in Fort Cochin or Mattancherry. Budget accommodation can be found in mainland Ernakulum.

Indian Airlines has daily flights to Bangalore, Mumbai, Delhi, Goa and Chennai. If flying is outside your budget, there's a whole bevy of buses that leave Kochi at regular intervals and fan out in every direction except seaward. You can easily get to any of the outlying regions either by state-owned or privately owned bus, but there are no advance reservations. Turn up, join the scrum and hope for the best, which in this case would be a seat. Failing this, try the railway station which has trains zipping up the coast to major destinations on a daily basis.

CHAPTER 22
Prime Ministers of India

Jawaharlal Nehru

Aug. 15,1947 - May 27,1964

Gulzari Lal Nanda

May 27,1964 -June 9,1964 (Interim) January 11 - 24,1966 (Interim)

Lal Bahadur Shastri

June 9,1964- January 11,1966

Indira Gandhi

Jan. 24,1966 to March 24,1977
Jan. 14,1980 to Oct. 31,1984

Morarji Desai

March 24,1977 to July 28,1979

Charan Singh

July 28,1979-Jan. 14,1980

Rajiv Gandhi

Oct. 31,1984 to Dec. 1,1989

V. P. Singh

Dec. 2,1989-Nov. 10,1990

Chandra Shekhar

Nov. 10,1990-June 21, 1991

P. V. Narasimha Rao

June 21,1991 to May 10,1996

Atal Bihari Vajpayee

May 16 to June 1,1996

H. D. Deve Gowda

June 1,1996 to April 21,1997

I. K. Gujral

April 21, 1997 - Nov. 28. 1997.

Atal Bihari Vajpayee

March 19, 1998 to 1999

Dr. Manmohan Singh

May 22, 2004 to 2014

Narendra Damodardas Modi

May 26, 2014 till date

CHAPTER 23
The Presidents of India

Dr. Rajendra Prasad

Jan. 26, 1950 to May 13,1962

Dr. Sarvepalli Radhakrishnan

(May 13,1962 to May 13,1967)

Dr. Zakir Hussain

(May 13,1967 to May 3, 1969)

Varahagiri Venkatagiri

(May 3,1969 to July 20, 1969)(acting)

Justice Mohammed Hidayatullah

July 20,1969 to August 24, 1969)(acting)

Varahagiri Venkatagiri

(August 24,1969 to August 24,1974)

Fakhruddin Ali Ahmed
(August 24, 1974 to Feb. 11, 1977)
B.D. Jatti
(Feb. 12,1977 to July 25,1977) (acting)
Neelam Sanjeeva Reddy

(July 25,1977 to July 25,1982)
Giani Zail Singh
(July 25,1982 to July 25,1987)
R. Venkataraman

(July 25, 1987 to July 25,1992)
Dr. Shanker Dayal Sharma
(July 25,1992 to July 25,1997)
K. R. Narayanan
July 25,1997-July 25, 2002)

A.P.J. Abdul Kalam

July 25, 2002 -2007

Mrs. Pratibha Patil

July 25 2007-2012

Pranab Mukherjee

July 25 2012 -2017

Ram Nath Kovind

July 25 2017- till date